The British Museum

ORIGAMI, POEMS AND PICTURES

With special thanks to Yoko Takenami, the Japan Society, Hannah Wiltshier, Nick Robinson,
the British Origami Society, and Timothy Clark at the British Museum for their contributions and advice.

First published 2017 by Nosy Crow Ltd
The Crow's Nest, 10a Lant Street
London SE1 1QR
www.nosycrow.com

ISBN 978 0 85763 938 7

Published in collaboration with the British Museum
All photographs © The Trustees of the British Museum
Text © Nosy Crow 2017
Origami diagrams and instructions © Nick Robinson 2017
Crab and grasshopper origami design by Nick Robinson
Dragonfly origami design by Kunihiko Kasahara
All other designs are traditional
Rabbit haiku translation © Ueda Makoto 1976, reprinted with the kind permission of University of Toronto Press
All other haiku translations © RH Blyth 1952
Every effort has been made to secure permission for the haiku translations. Any errors or omissions
will be corrected in subsequent editions provided notification is sent to the publisher.
All rights reserved.

A CIP catalogue record for this book is available from the British Library.

Printed in Turkey.
Papers used by Nosy Crow are made from wood
grown in sustainable forests.

1 3 5 7 9 8 6 4 2

JAPAN is a beautiful country with many special traditions. This book brings together three of the most highly celebrated Japanese arts and crafts: origami, haiku poetry and painting.

ORIGAMI is the ancient Japanese art of paper folding. It is believed that paper was first invented in China, in 105 AD; however, many people believe that paper is even older than this. Paper was brought to Japan around 500 AD by Buddhist monks. In Japan, folding paper soon became an art form. At first it was used mostly in religious ceremonies, because paper was so expensive and most people could not afford to buy it. Origami was also used to create paper butterflies for wedding ceremonies. By the 1600s, play-origami was used throughout Japan and had come to Europe as well. Today it is enjoyed by people around the world as a craft that is both beautiful and fun.

HAIKU is one of the world's oldest forms of poetry. It evolved over several hundred years and by the late 1600s, the most famous haiku poet, Bashō, began writing his simple, elegant poems. Inspired by Zen Buddhism, his poems – along with those of Buson, Issa and many others – celebrated nature and everyday objects, and attempted to capture a moment in time. Western haiku follows a pattern of three lines, the first with five syllables, the second with seven and the third with five, but in Japan, haiku is traditionally more fluid and often includes another two lines at the end. The translations in this book have different numbers of syllables because they were made as faithfully as possible to the original Japanese words. However many syllables each poem has, haiku poetry is some of the most beautiful in the world.

PICTURES of nature and animals are an important part of Japanese art, and the British Museum has an amazing collection of many thousands of Japanese paintings, woodcuts and prints. One of the most celebrated Japanese artists in the collection is Katsushika Hokusai, who lived from 1760–1849, and is considered by many to be the greatest artist of the Edo period. His masterpiece was a series of woodcuts called 'Thirty-six views of Mount Fuji', of which the best-known print is 'The Great Wave', which influenced Western artists such as Whistler, van Gogh and Monet. The lovely pictures in this book are by many different Japanese artists, including Utagawa Hiroshige and Kitagawa Utamaro. Their art feels as beautiful today as it did when it was first created hundreds of years ago.

We hope that this book will inspire you to learn more about Japan and its arts and crafts. Write a poem, paint a picture, make some origami — and explore your own creativity!

Make a paper **BOAT**

舟

FUNE

BOAT

how long the day:
the boat is talking
with the shore.
— SOKAN

1. Start with a square, patterned side facing up. Fold in half upwards (valley fold).

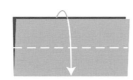

2. Fold the rectangle in half downwards.

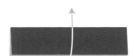

3. Lift up the top single layer.

4. This is the result. Now turn the paper over.

5. Fold all corners (all layers) to lie on the horizontal crease.

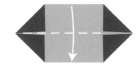

6. Fold the top half downwards and open from the middle.

7. Now your boat is finished!

Make a paper FROG

the old pond,
a frog jumps in —
the sound of water.
— BASHŌ

蛙

KAERU

FROG

  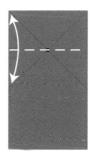   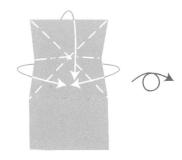

1. Fold a square in half, patterned side facing up. Fold the upper right corner down to the left vertical edge, crease and unfold.

2. Fold the upper left corner down to the right vertical edge, crease and unfold to form an 'X' in the centre.

3. Fold the upper edge down to meet the bottom edge, crease and unfold. Now turn over.

4. Press the outside edges of the horizontal crease towards the middle to fold the sides inwards and the top edge down. Now turn over.

 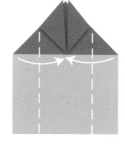  

5. Fold the loose corners to the top corner of the triangle.

6. Fold the sides to the centre. Rotate the paper to the right.

7. Make a gentle 'S' curve on the underside of the frog (fold without making a crease).

8. Now your frog is finished! Press the bend gently, then release quickly to watch it hop!

Make a paper FAN

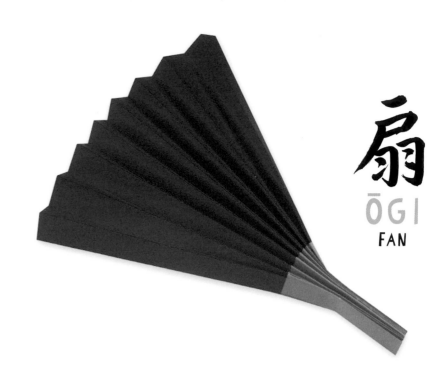

扇

ŌGI

FAN

> a handle
> on the moon —
> and what a splendid fan.
> — SOKAN

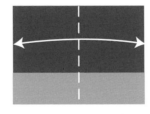

1. Start with a square, patterned side facing up. Fold the lower edge to about half way up the paper.

2. Fold in half from side to side, crease and unfold.

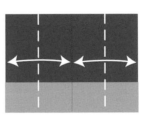

3. Fold outer edges to the vertical centre, crease and unfold. Rotate paper to the right.

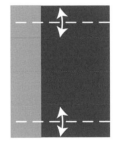

4. Valley fold the bottom edge up to meet the nearest crease line.

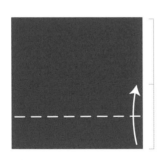

5. Unfold and repeat step 4. Unfold again and mountain fold along the same crease.

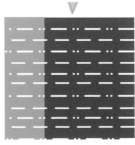

6. From the bottom, pleat the paper into equal sections using mountain and valley folds. The mountain folds happen along exisiting fold lines.

7. Hold near the base, then spread out the pleats.

8. Now your fan is finished!

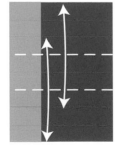

Make a paper CRAB

蟹
KANI
CRAB

a tiny crablet
climbs up my legs
in the clear water.
– BASHŌ

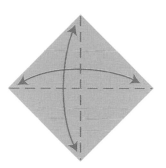

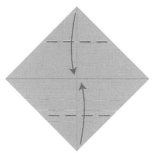

1. Start with the plain side upwards, crease and unfold both diagonals.

2. Fold upper and lower corners to the centre.

3. Fold the corners out at a slight angle, in opposite directions, so the tips stick out slightly.

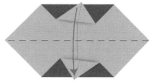

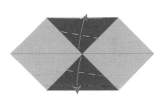

4. Fold in half downwards.

5. Fold two flaps down. The exact angle isn't important.

6. Fold two corners behind.

7. Crease the front tips to point downwards.

8. Now your crab is finished!

Make a paper FISH

魚

SAKANA
FISH

the little fish carried backwards in the clear water.
— KITO

1. Start with a square, plain side upwards, crease and unfold both diagonals. Turn the paper over.

2. Fold each corner to the centre, crease and unfold. Turn the paper over.

3. Fold each outer edge to the centre, crease and unfold.

4. Fold the sides inwards as you fold the upper edge down. Push against the folds to collapse the paper inwards along the creases.

5. Repeat on the lower edge.

6. Fold the two lower flaps down to meet in the middle.

7. Fold the lower left flap up to the right.

8. Fold the same flap back on itself to the left.

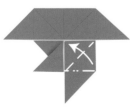

9. Repeat the last two steps on the right side.

10. Leaving a small gap, fold the upper flaps down at 45 degrees to meet in the middle.

11. This is the result. Turn the paper over and rotate it.

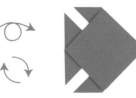

12. Now your fish is finished!

Make a paper RABBIT

even the rabbit droops one
of her ears —
midsummer heat!
— SHIKI

兎

USAGI

RABBIT

Start
with steps
1– 4 of
the Fish.

1. Fold the bottom
corners up and in
towards the centre fold.

2. Fold in half from
left to right. Rotate
anti-clockwise.

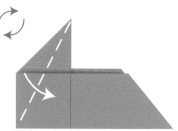

3. Fold from the lower
left corner to just below
the top of the ear.

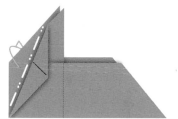

4. Repeat on
the reverse.

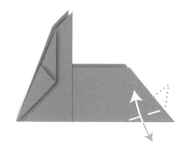

5. Fold the tail over,
crease and unfold.

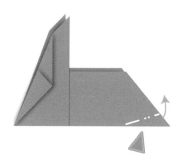

6. Reverse the
tail inside.

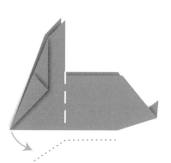

7. Fold the body
at a slight angle
so it will stand up.

8. Now your
rabbit is finished!

Make a paper BUTTERFLY

蝶々

CHŌCHŌ
BUTTERFLY

> o butterfly,
> what are you dreaming there,
> fanning your wings?
> — CHIYO-NI

Start with steps 1–5 of the Fish.

1. Fold the upper half behind.

2. Fold both top flaps down to make a triangle.

3. Fold two corners inwards.

4. This is the result. Turn the paper over.

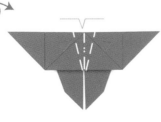

5. Fold the wings together to create a sharp centre line then unfold. Pinch the sides together to form a triangular ridge.

6. Now your butterfly is finished!

Make a paper **BIRD**

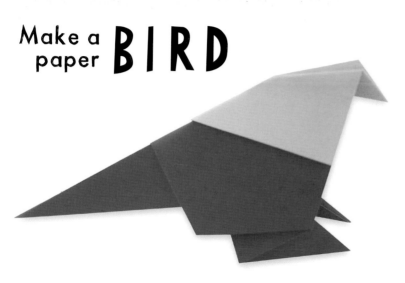

鳥

TORI

BIRD

DIFFICULTY ● ● ●

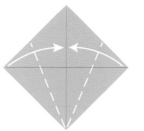  

1. Start with a square, plain side upwards. Crease along both diagonals. Fold both lower edges to the vertical centre crease. Turn the paper over.

2. Fold down the upper triangle. Turn the paper over again.

3. Fold both halves of the upper edge to meet the vertical centre. Crease and unfold.

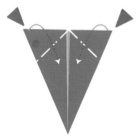   

4. Peel back the top layer of paper to tuck the outer corners into the centre.

5. Fold both flaps down as far as possible.

6. Fold the lower points up to line up with the existing creases.

7. Make a pleat partway down the lower triangle, using a valley and mountain crease.

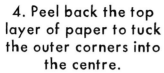   

8. Fold in half from left to right. Rotate the paper.

9. Tuck and fold the point inside to form a beak.

10. Now your bird is finished!

Make a paper DRAGONFLY

蜻蛉

TONBO

DRAGONFLY

You'll need scissors for this one. Please ask a grown-up if you need help!

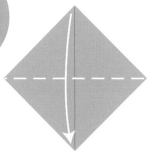

1. Start with the plain side upwards and fold in half left to right. Crease and unfold, then fold in half downwards.

2. Fold left and right corners to the bottom corner.

3. Fold the lower edges to the vertical centre. Crease and unfold.

4. Reverse the flaps by tucking them inside themselves.

5. Fold the narrow flaps outwards to create a straight horizontal line.

6. This is the result. Turn the paper over.

7. Fold the right edge to the vertical centre, carefully squashing the hidden corner flat.

8. This is the result. Repeat on the left side.

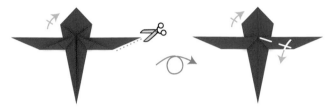

9. Cut through both layers along the dotted line. Repeat on the left side.

10. Turn over and fold the top half of the flap down. Repeat on the other side.

11. Now your dragonfly is finished!

Make a paper GRASSHOPPER

飛蝗

BATTA
GRASSHOPPER

grasshopper —
do not trample to pieces
the pearls of bright dew.
— ISSA

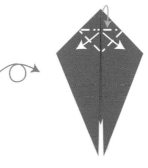

Start with steps 1 – 4 of the Dragonfly.

1. Turn the paper over.

2. Fold the top corner to the dotted line, crease and unfold. Make a tiny, narrow pleat on the lower flap.

3. Make another tiny, narrow pleat. Turn the paper over.

4. Fold the top point down, crease and unfold. Then open out and fold down to make a small rectangle.

5. Fold the right half underneath. Rotate the paper anti-clockwise.

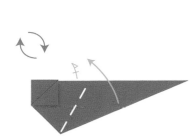

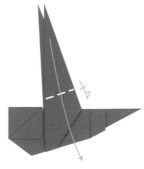

6. Fold both leg flaps upwards.

7. Fold both legs down again at an angle.

8. Fold the lower edge inside. Repeat underneath.

9. Fold a corner over to form an eye. Repeat underneath.

10. Now your grasshopper is finished!

DIFFICULTY ● ● ●

Make a paper HORSE

We gaze
Even at horses,
This morn of snow.
– BASHŌ

馬
UMA
HORSE

DIFFICULTY ●●●

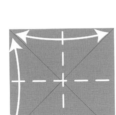

1. Start with a square, patterned side upwards, crease and unfold both diagonals. Turn the paper over.

2. Fold in half from side to side, crease and unfold, in both directions.

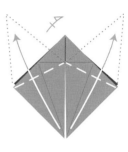

3. Use these creases to tuck the sides inwards and fold the top edge down.

4. Keeping the open end towards the bottom, fold the lower edges to the centre fold, and unfold.

5. Repeat on the reverse. Fold the triangular flap down and then unfold.

6. Cut through the top layer where shown. Turn the paper over and repeat the cut on the other side.

7. Fold two layers upwards. Repeat on reverse.

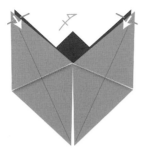

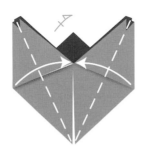

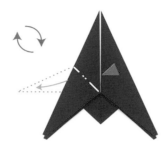

8. Fold the tips of the flaps down. Repeat on reverse.

9. Fold the top layer of outer edges to the centre fold. Repeat on reverse and rotate the paper upside down.

10. Fold the top left piece down towards the left along the dotted line. Unfold and tuck inside to make the shape 3D.

11. Make a smaller fold on the right side, unfold and tuck inside to create a 3D head.

12. Now your horse is finished!

Make a paper FLOWER

> Under the cherry-blossoms
> None are
> Utter strangers
> — ISSA

HANA
FLOWER

Start with steps 1–3 of the Horse.

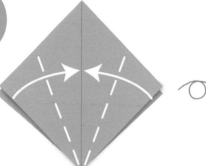

1. Rotate it 180 degrees so the open end is towards the top. Fold the top layer of the lower edges in towards the vertical centre.

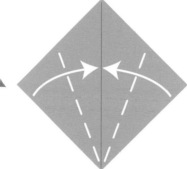

2. Turn the paper over and repeat the last step.

3. Fold a single layer to the right.

4. Fold the lower layer behind.

5. Fold to match the dotted line, crease and unfold. Turn over and repeat on the reverse.

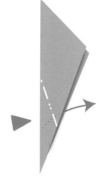

6. Open out and tuck the flap back between the layers.

7. Hold near the base and gently unfold the layers at the top to make the petals.

8. Now your flower is finished!

Make a paper CRANE

it's play for the cranes
flying up to the clouds
the year's first sunrise
– CHIYO-NI

鶴
TSURU
CRANE

Start with steps 1–5 of the Horse.

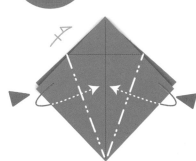

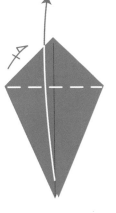

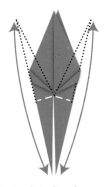

1. Open out and then tuck the corners back inside and repeat behind.

2. Fold a lower corner all the way up. Repeat behind.

3. Fold two lower edges to the centre. Repeat behind.

4. Fold the lower flaps up to meet the dotted lines. Crease and unfold.

5. Reverse the same flaps inside themselves.

6. Reverse fold to form a beak.

7. Fold the wings down. You can pull the wings gently apart to make the centre 3D.

8. Now your crane is finished!

INDEX

Boat
Woodblock print titled 'Kanagawa-oki nami-ura' (The Great Wave)
by Katsushika Hokusai
1831

Boat haiku by Yamasaki Sokan
(1465–1553)

Fish
Woodblock print of a carp
by Chikuseki
About 1900

Fish haiku by Kitō
(1741–1789)

Frog
Woodblock print of a frog by a pond
by Ogata Gekko
1859–1920

Frog haiku by Matsuo Bashō
(1644–1694)

Rabbit
Rabbits (detail), from a handscroll of Japanese subjects
by Kawamura Bunpo
1779–1821

Rabbit haiku by Akutagawa
Ryünosuke (1892–1927)

Fan
Woodblock print of fans
by Utagawa Hiroshige II
1826–1869

Fan haiku by Yamasaki Sokan
(1465–1553)

Butterfly
Woodblock print of flowers, peonies and butterfly
by Katsushika Hokusai
Mid-1830s

Butterfly haiku by Fukuda
Chiyo-ni (1703–1775)

Crab
Woodblock print of a crab and fish
by Utagawa Hiroshige
About 1832–1842

Crab haiku by Matsuo Bashō
(1644–1694)

Bird
Woodblock print of a bullfinch and weeping cherry-tree
by Katsushika Hokusai
Mid-1830s

Bird haiku by Uejima Onitsura
(1661–1738)

Dragonfly
Woodblock print of a dragonfly
by Morita Kak?
1870–1931

Dragonfly haiku by Nikyu
(dates unknown)

Flower
Woodblock print of cherry blossom
by Utagawa Hiroshige
1847–1852

Cherry blossom haiku by Kobayashi Issa
(1762–1826)

Grasshopper
Woodblock print of a grasshopper
by Kitagawa Utamaro
1753–1806

Grasshopper haiku by Kobayashi Issa
(1762–1826)

Crane
Woodblock print of Mount Fuji
by Katsushika Hokusai
1831

Crane haiku by Fukuda Chiyo-ni
(1703–1775)

Horse
Woodblock print of a cavalry officer on horseback
by Katsushika Hokusai
About 1833–1834

Horse haiku by Matsuo Bashō
(1644–1694)

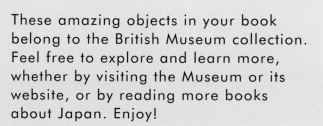

Scan this **QR code** on your smart phone to find out more about these objects!

These amazing objects in your book belong to the British Museum collection. Feel free to explore and learn more, whether by visiting the Museum or its website, or by reading more books about Japan. Enjoy!

FOLDS AND SYMBOLS

Here are some helpful hints and tips to follow when making your origami models.

TIPS:

○ Make sure your paper is the correct shape for each project. Most will need square paper. To make a rectangle, fold a square in half or cut the paper in half.

○ Always fold on a flat surface and make sure your folds are neat. Press your folds in place by running your fingernail along them.

○ This book starts with the simplest projects, and gradually gets trickier. Look out for the difficulty level on each page.

○ If you don't get it right the first time, don't give up! Origami takes lots of practice and your projects will get better and better.

This book includes beautiful patterned paper, so the instructions refer to the 'patterned side'. For clarity, the diagrams have been created using a darker tone to represent the patterned side of the paper. If you choose to make more models using plain origami paper, please substitute the dark side for 'patterned side' and the pale side for 'plain side'.

LINES:

— — — — — —
Dashed line:
Fold the paper forwards
(also called a 'valley fold')

— ·· — ·· — ·· —
Dashed and dotted line:
Fold the paper backwards
(also called a 'mountain fold')

————————
Straight line: Creased line

·····················
Dotted line:
Your fold should
follow this shape

ARROWS:

→
Fold in this direction

↰
Fold behind

▷ ◁
Tuck a fold inside

⇨
Unfold

↻
Turn the paper over

↺
Rotate the paper

⤵
Step fold/pleat

TYPES OF FOLD:

Valley fold: Fold the paper so that the crease is at the bottom and the paper is folded forward into itself.

Mountain fold: Fold the paper so that the crease is at the top and the paper is folded behind itself.

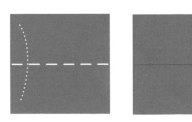

Valley and unfold

DIFFICULTY LEVELS   Simple ● ○ ○   Medium ● ● ○   Tricky ● ● ●

8 up Poner time Hale
was a Big dractioor

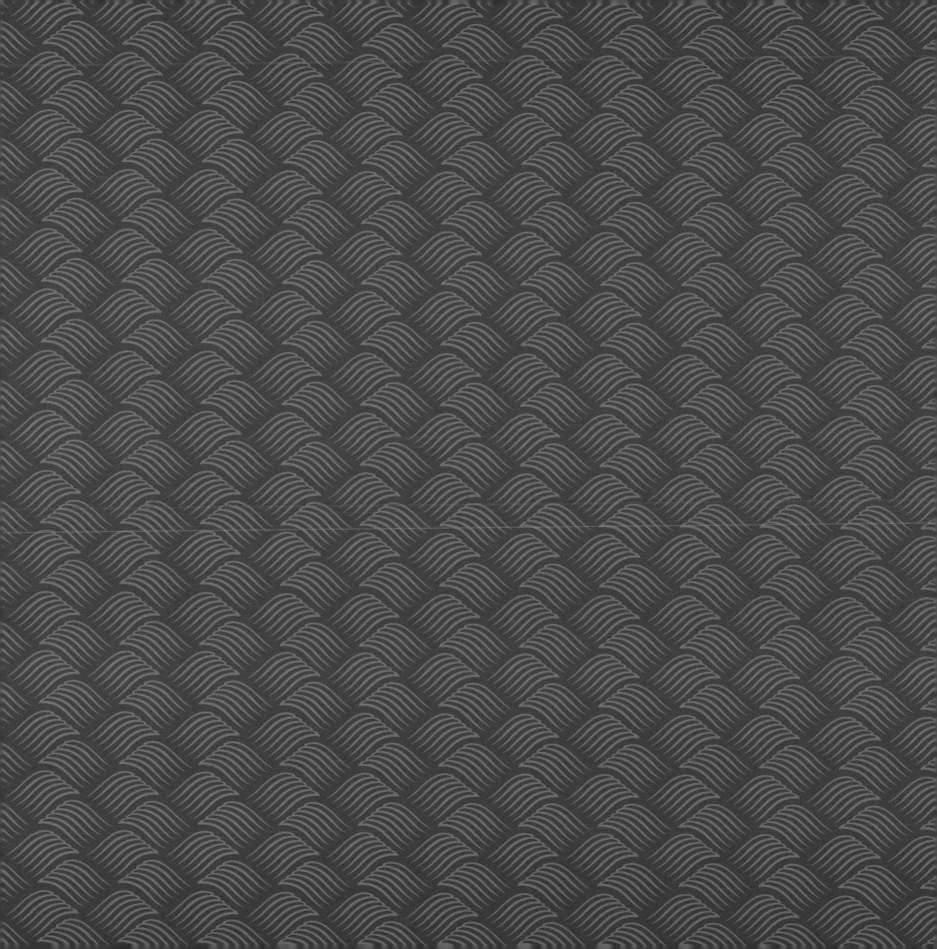